WAVE IF YOU CAN SEE ME

WAVE IF YOU CAN SEE ME

Poems

Susan Ludvigson

Red Hen Press | *Pasadena, CA*

Book layout by Mark E. Cull

Library of Congress Cataloging-in-Publication Data

Names: Ludvigson, Susan, author.
Title: Wave if you can see me : poems / Susan Ludvigson.
Description: First edition. | Pasadena, CA : Red Hen Press, [2020]
Identifiers: LCCN 2020025810 (print) | LCCN 2020025811 (ebook) | ISBN
    9781597098632 (trade paperback) | ISBN 9781597098649 (epub)
Subjects: LCSH: Bereavement—Poetry. | LCGFT: Poetry.
Classification: LCC PS3562.U27 W38 2020 (print) | LCC PS3562.U27 (ebook)
    | DDC 811/.54—dc23
LC record available at https://lccn.loc.gov/2020025810
LC ebook record available at https://lccn.loc.gov/2020025811

The National Endowment for the Arts, the Los Angeles County Arts Commission, the Ahmanson Foundation, the Dwight Stuart Youth Fund, the Max Factor Family Foundation, the Pasadena Tournament of Roses Foundation, the Pasadena Arts & Culture Commission and the City of Pasadena Cultural Affairs Division, the City of Los Angeles Department of Cultural Affairs, the Audrey & Sydney Irmas Charitable Foundation, the Kinder Morgan Foundation, the Meta & George Rosenberg Foundation, the Albert and Elaine Borchard Foundation, the Adams Family Foundation, the Riordan Foundation, Amazon Literary Partnership, and the Mara W. Breech Foundation partially support Red Hen Press.

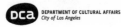

First Edition
Published by Red Hen Press
www.redhen.org

ACKNOWLEDGMENTS

Sincere gratitude goes to the editors of the journals in which these poems first appeared:

Apple Valley Review: "Closing In"; *Big River Poetry*: "I Want to Say Something"; *Cold Mountain Review*: "Begin with Water Crystals," "Ghost Animals," "Grace"; *Connotation Press*: "Remote Viewing," "The Seven Villages"; *Five Points*: "First Love," "Mythologies," "Sharing the Territory"; *Georgia Review*: "You Could Be Drinking Faulkner's Bourbon"; *One*: "Since You Died"; *Poet's Calendar*: "A Christmas of Cockatiels"; *Southern Review*: "Prism," "How it Can Happen," "From the Cabin's Porch"; *Story South*: "At Night When the Music Comes"; and *Yale Review*: "Nightshirt Sonata."

Wave If You Can See Me was the 2013 winner of the James Dickey Prize from *Five Points*.

I would like to thank poets Julie Funderburk, Lucinda Grey, Patricia Hooper, Kathryn Kirkpatrick, Dannye Powell, Katherine Soniat, Julie Suk, and Dede Wilson for their generosity, astute critical observations and friendship.

In Loving Memory of James Scott Ely, 1944–1988.

Contents

3

4

LIGHTING THE SPIRIT

That's what I'm after—

I want it to gleam
no matter how much
pain infuses it.

I want it to shine as if a lamp
were under it, or fire,
like something molten under the crust of earth. Like stars
burning through the debris of history,
like love burning through the dark of loss.

1

He will say: "I crossed my own mountains into others because it was asked of me, asked as inaudibly as a finger laid on the lips for silence, but to which the blood gave answer . . ."

—Kay Boyle,
"The Invitation In It"
American Citizen

From the Cabin's Porch,
Overlooking the Edisto River, April

for Patty

I read your poems,
surprised by the grief loosening
in me.

Through the screen, I fix my eyes on a cypress,
Spanish moss lifts and falls like gauze
in the breeze.

A rattle of clothespins in a bag,
in a wicker basket, a pileated woodpecker
drilling a pine.

Calls of cardinals float by, ripples
on the river.

Snow collapses the lilacs, though you don't mention lilacs.

Driving down, I felt a calm that bordered
on exultation. The world apple-green,
full of promise. No one I loved
was dying. I even thought, *If this peace
is a sign of my mind's going, so be it,*
knowing acceptance would last about as long
as it did, my husband confiding his fears
at breakfast, before loading the canoe.

Que sera, sera,
I think of our mothers in their gardens,
their trumpet-flower flirtations, how suddenly
sheets snapped in the wind,
then froze.

WOMAN AT THE WINDOW

Caspar David Friedrich, Oil on Canvas, 1822

The way she leans, her whole body
transfixed by what she sees, or
what she's looking at or looking for
through the opened shutter, I have
to think there's someone coming,
or someone going, for the mast
of a sailboat appears, too close
to the house, this side of the woods,
to make sense, yet it's all there, tall,
looming far above even
the upper window, seeming
to rise from the garden. No Elbe
in sight, just the rigging that says
it must be there. The greens
and browns of her velvet dress,
the muted greens of the walls and shutters,
the golden brown of her slippers,
the pale mast as her husband paints them,
almost convince. Does he believe the boat
or concoct it from her imagination?
Whose longing determines
the tenderness of the illusion,
the intensity of the stance?

How It Can Happen

You've had to flee to another country.
I go with you,
but not all the way to your destination.
I wait in a dark house while you are taken
to a secret location.
We knew this could happen.

An old man appears where I'm staying,
knowing everything. He is shaking with fear.
Someone gives me instructions.
The street is dark. Shadows
and other people's dogs. We never thought
things would go this far.
We always expected, unreasonably, to escape.

Mythologies

Think of the people who bid at Sotheby's
on objects that belonged to dead
celebrities—a baseball cap, a '30s lamp,
a silver clock, a palette of paints—
as if having them confers
their owners' glamour.

I must admit I'm guilty,
enchanted by twin cupboards I found
at a *brocante* that came from the Deux Magots
in the twenties. Who knows,
Hemingway might've brushed against them!
Zelda could have admired the sculpted panels,
run her finger along the Griffiths and scrolls.

I have better tools, yet use my mother's old
wooden spoons and rusty iron butcher knife,
her rolling pin and salad molds for things other
than her old recipes, but sometimes
her recipes too. Maybe I'm imagining her DNA
still clinging to them, recognizing mine.

My husband took it another direction.
Remembering his mother's prohibition
against sitting on her pink Victorian sofa,
he would have put it on the street despite
my objections, until we made love
on the pristine velvet, staining and redeeming it.
One of the dogs tore out half the stuffing
from underneath. Another put teeth marks
in the fruitwood frame, and slept on it

nightly, replacing its vague perfume
with his Spaniel scent. Then my husband
wouldn't part with it.

REMOTE VIEWING

Remote Viewing is a mental faculty that allows a perceiver (a "viewer")
to describe or give details about a target that is inaccessible to normal
sense due to distance, time, or shielding. . . . From this explanation,
it is obvious that remote viewing is related to so-called psi phenomena.
　　　　　　　　　—Paul H. Smith, "What is Remote Viewing?"

Say I know you're in Rome
where it's two in the afternoon.
I'm in my garden concentrating on a fire ant
venturing farther from his nest than his cohorts,
dizzying the dogs. In the background I make out
a shape that might be fountain or rose window.
In my notebook, I draw water pouring from a pump
and see you sitting on the lip of heaven, but I know
that can't be because it's Rome, so I try again—
you're sitting at a café table near a waterfall
where what tumbles seems a torrent of syllables
shaped like lips and birds. One of the dogs
begins to yip in tune with something
I can't hear, and you're suddenly clear as glass,
laughing.

At Night When the Music Comes

I listen as if I'm waiting for clues
to my life, now it's a choral piece,
piano accompaniment—
I can't make out the words but tenors
and sopranos urge me somewhere
forward as if toward doors that might
open, increasing the volume
so I don't have to strain to hear,
but then it's a cappella until the whole
thing switches to orchestra,
horns taking the lead, though
if I were choosing it would be strings,
and despite the lack of spasms
that could suggest tumor or injury, I suspect
Nietzsche is right: music
is in the muscles, which doesn't explain
why it happens on the way to sleep,
the body letting go until
I stop to check the clock
or decide to listen harder,
sometimes rewarded by a phrase
that seems familiar, although I'm never
sure, especially when it's interrupted by the dogs
stirring in their crates or a car
going by, even when it picks up where it left off,
keeping its own time, simply
letting me eavesdrop, and while some say
it's tooth fillings picking up radio signals,
I'd rather think of the brain
tuning to frequencies closer to invention
than explicable chance—but then, the two
are intimates, aren't they, and shouldn't I
just let them dance?

Closing In

Mist closing over the mountains,
the balcony becomes a secret garden,
ruffled petunias and moss roses
the only color in the planter, even the small table
and chairs disappearing against the white
of walls and the silver beyond.
Miniature paradise of a certain kind, yet

look at the invisibility I could walk into.
Who hasn't felt the draw, the chosen
loneliness of forests, the wish
to enter an abandoned cabin,
to find a plate, a spoon, wild gooseberries
growing in a patch of rocky soil.

A pale wedge of gray begins, backlights
the highest peak, a hazy silhouette
that means the world may soon
return to itself. But

I don't want the reemergence
of the roof across the road, the high relief
of perspective. I want to find a bed
with a ragged quilt, a root cellar,
shelves of preserves that might have been there
five or fifty years.

The trees grow so close, ancient
paths are mostly obscured. It's dark
at what might be noon. If I kept walking,
what then? The wish for a secret garden?
Love in the house where I left it?

2

And I walk where I want
in this strange land, attempting
to stare with no memory
when the black hawk descends
to the neck of the hare.

— Kathryn Stripling Byer,
"Search Party – 3,"
The Girl in the Midst of the Harvest

From the Window, the Marina

Whites and blues perfectly
still against a steel wool sky
and water bordered by summer marsh grass,
parentheses around the river. Blocks
away my husband is being infused
with toxins meant to cure him.

An owl sits on a trellis over the ramp to the dock.
His job, though he is neither flesh nor feathered,
is to scare the gulls from the pristine walkway.
He's as passive as the water I have to look at hard
to see a hint of ripple. This might be a still life except
for the occasional pelican flying high above a faint
ruffling of palm. My husband calls from the hospital

to ask how I am. I'm in the hotel, napping,
waking, staring out the window,
nursing a stomach upset by too much wine
and worry. How can I whine
about my body's minor rebellions
when he is grateful for the poisons that might save him,
for the time to write stories he's dreaming up even now.

A boat is gliding out, someone walks the planks
where the owl keeps vigil. A breeze picks up,
bending the grasses. Cars begin crossing the bridge
that had been empty all morning, and the clouds
start scrubbing the air until some blue leaks through.

DARKER THAN BEFORE

This year the nights grow darker than before,
when you were here. Panicked by demons, you reached
for what you'd hidden just behind a door—

the closet farther than the window, more
time to think before you'd have to breach
a year grown darker than the one before.

Once, sleepless, I climbed to the second floor
to paint. Halfway back down a stair creaked—
an instant—you alert behind the door.

I heard the click, cried out so you would hear
my voice, breaking with fear. Now I sleep
sometimes through nights still darker than before

you died. You'd mapped and set off flares in war,
seen riddled bodies, moving grasses creeping
close to where you were hiding. Behind a door,

the weapon you kept closeted, and for
an instant thought me Viet Cong slipping
through a night darker than before. You,
ready. Cocked gun behind the door.

Always Paris

late late suitcases not packed no
tickets haven't written home
or called in months in years
meet Mary at La Closerie de Lilas
pink clouds follow the falling sun
dusty air glowing mid-beer maybe
it's today I should have left call
Drusilla Linda Carol stroll
Blvd. St. Germain stopping to buy
lilies on the way to Mimi's where
across the river a symphony someone
singing a voice so pure and light it drifts
across like yes like silk Gianne think
home the ones who worry there
and back in my tiny flat look
at shelves two stories high filled
with clothes and pots and pans
and canned tomatoes cassoulet
and peas decide to leave the food still
the suitcase will not close look across
the courtyard a building under
renovation new apartments
being sold listen through the window
hammering whistling still not
dressed close the window now
in shadow in the glass who is
she red hair fallen from her crown
where it was pinned dreaming
a garden walled by blooming
lilacs Mary gone Mother gone where who
does she think she is

Ghost Animals

We knew they were out there at dusk,
all that bamboo for cover, to say nothing
of the thick forsythia, distracting the eye
with its yellow flags. You know they're there
when the owls come out, telling each other
across the yards, and when the dogs
come slithering through their hatch door,
heads down and quiet. It's then
I head for the cabin.
                              I suspect they slip in
through the side window. I turn on
the lamps, not the overhead light, and say,
"Welcome." I don't want to scare them.
My "Spirit House" Mary called it, and I take
it on trust. Whatever animal comes unbidden
and invisible must have something to tell
or something to ask. I wait for the words
that can't be spoken.

I Want to Say Something

I want to say something about connection,
but what come to mind are some of my mother's
unwieldy sweaters, the yarn too loose
for the pattern, or her skills too loose
for the yarn, how sometimes they'd grow
into garments that might fit a five-hundred-pound man
and still be baggy.

This is the way I picture the universe,
an infinity of stitches, each somehow entwined
with whatever it is that makes a whole, but the pattern
impenetrable and earth herself a miniscule morsel of frizz
in an ever-expanding sleeve, the decorative whorl we've seen
in photos from our moon likely invisible
to anyone else in the cosmos. Each particle
of murderer, priest, child, of each extinct horse
and tortoise and bone we can't identify, linked.

The idea that we're part of it,
the evolving earth and all her kin
into infinity, holds me.
The stitches can all be in place, the purling
perfection, but somehow the whole
grows too large for anyone we know.

I Am Trying to Tell You Something

I know—everything on this side must now
seem pale or irrelevant. And my words wander,
confused under the fur of dream and dogs
and disorder.

You should see the mess
the new owner of the house next door has made.
Yes, he's painted the window frames
blue, but the porch is littered
with boards and debris
and he's scraped the lawn to pale dirt
and red clay. Cut down too many trees. I wish
you'd send word how long I should stay.

The new fountain a short two blocks away
might impress you, and some
of the neighborhood renovations—Victorians
coquettish with colors they haven't worn
in decades.

Of course the dogs complain
about the things we don't do without you,
but settle for sleeping on the bed. Everything's
a trade-off. As you knew.

I should be paying bills instead of writing you.
I should be making lists. I'm not letting myself
paint or frame until I've done the chores I hate.

When I'm not talking to you, I talk to the crow
on the mantel. Try to cultivate the live ones
in the backyard, but so far no luck. I keep

the radio on, but don't sing along.
I fill our rooms with orchids—some, gifts
from when you died, are still alive—others
new. The caladium on the table is tired,
far past its prime.

Love, it rains all the time.

In the Country of Birds and Wild Animals

I walk with a cockatiel on each shoulder,
while a tiger slips through tall grasses,
leaps stalks of elephant-ears, a silent music
in the line he draws on air.
You, in khaki, carry a hawk on your wrist,
nod to me from a distance.
When one of my cockatiels disappears,
I weep with grief deeper than bird-loss. You tell me
it may have been your hawk who snatched
and ate it, but you'll help me look,
and you do, into dry fields
with broken-down buildings.
I follow you back to the wilderness
of jungle, its soft green shadows.

The cockatiel returns, and again I have one
on each shoulder—then another pair
of smaller birds, finches, both singing. You smile
as if the world were unchanged, and you
had nothing to do with it, though peace and joy
have reentered the garden.

Moving Toward the Margins

out from the body
of the text, into a place that looks
like nothingness,
slipping from the ends
of lines into that pristine space
beyond words. Now the world falls
away

                  and here I am on the frozen
pond of childhood, the rink frozen
beyond its limits, light dimming
where I spin out, bending
into swan-dive,
a single blade propelling me
toward what I can't see.

3

It's true: with you gone, even the sky grieves.
This is to say love burns, but at a distance
Like a star.

— Kelly Cherry,
" I Went to Find You,"
Death and Transfiguration

. . . if you could make the leap
from wherever you are to wherever I am, you'd see the press of fear
in each brushstroke, the sad lack of scope.

—David Harsent,
"Marriage – XXVII,"
Marriage

GOETHE AT THE WINDOW OF HIS ROOM IN ROME

*Johann Heinrich Wilhelm Tischbein,
1787, watercolor, chalk and pen and ink
over graphite on paper.*

The window is narrow, and so is he,
the walls dark, his figure gray, shirt
unbuttoned in the back, the room
empty. He's slouched, his posture seems
to say that everything's as bleak
as the room itself. Outside the light is bright,
as we'd expect—but all we see
is part of a roof across the way bleached
in sun, so the only view he has
is below, where in the cobbled street
something might be going on—a street fair
maybe, a woman with a blue parasol
or a comely man buying a pear.

We know a brain like his was constantly
churning, we think of poems and novels
and plays. We don't recall his passion
for drawing and painting, or that he thought
he'd be known for his color theory.

We can't know what he was feeling, standing
at the window, posing. But we can guess
that when he wrote, *Do you know
the land where the lemon trees bloom?*
he wasn't thinking of days like this one.

We Learn How the Brain Can Be Tricked

out of pain. A woman with a missing hand
puts her arms into a box, is told
to open and flex all ten fingers, to pretend
the absent hand is there. Her task is to watch
as mirrors in the box appear
to make both hands whole. Her mind is clear,
she knows about the mirror, yet
the brain believes the image,
relaxes its grip on the nerves. Her ghost
pain goes away as if it had never heard
of injury.

If an identical twin sees her sister
beaten, does she feel welts rise on her skin?
Can the body be deceived into empathy?

How to trigger the impulse that feels
the ache of a man
whose mind has gone awry—not the reflex
we all have had—there but for the grace of God go I—
but his emptiness burrowing in, so that we are
hollow with it.
It would change the world.

Could we, then, ask our minds
to enter another's happiness,
another's pleasures—

maybe a fragrant garden
with a frog pond, a shady bench,
the glow of a prize for achievement—
great sex?

Once, when I was young and in
wrong love, a wiser woman counseled,
Try to live it in your imagination. It sounded
pale, diluted, not to say impossible. But now
we know the brain
is capable of offering the body
what it wishes, what it needs.
We've just begun to find the keys.

After Your Death

It's night in a foreign country
that isn't anywhere we've been.
We're standing in front of buildings
in neglected neighborhoods.
You're anxious among the swarms of people
offering tastings of the local food.
I sit at a small table and eat the strange dishes,
one with a seafood I don't recognize,
as you slip away. I look and look, with the help
of some of the men, who lead me through
crowds, then back to the ancient apartments,
where I decide each is perfectly livable except
for the fallen stone and debris. A big dog
snarls as I pick my way through, surprising me.
You know how I always expect dogs to be friendly.
I'm still torn between thinking we could live here,
learn the language, and wanting to flee
to places I know you'd feel safer.
Someone claims to have spotted you, and I head
in that direction. I watch an old steamer
slide away in the distance,
wave as if you could see me.

Geel

It sounds like it might be found in a "hyperbolic universe,"
the kind we wouldn't recognize, curved like the space it's in,
so that we might imagine its inhabitants in sci-fi neon orange.
But no. It's a village in Belgium where every family
since the thirteenth century adopts a madman or woman.
He who would be outcast anywhere but there
sits at the table eating his portion of veal and potatoes,
waving his arms, railing at strangers the family can't see,
pacing the floor until the tile is worn, while someone walks at his side,
rubs his back when he sits, settles him with tea. Or she,
demure in her chair, embroidering a tablecloth, then
tossing dishes out the window, baring her teeth at neighbors,
accusing them of lacing her wine with antifreeze. She
is gently led to the garden, to sit in the shade near the roses.
Someone brushes her hair, hums to her, polishes her nails.

NUDES

I never thought I'd want to draw or paint them,
but here I am in a class making ugly marks
on paper and canvas, my eyes not speaking
to my hand, my hand not listening when they try.
It looks so easy. At home I meant to copy
what seemed a simple figure, and all my lines became
rough intersecting hills.

Odd to discover all I don't see
while intently looking. In one painting,
I completely forgot an arm. It wasn't until the next day
that I saw it was missing. It's like not noticing
the inner voice that's always whispering,
confusing what's happening on the outside
with what meanders through the mind.

The strangest of all is the wish to do this,
to make forms and shadows blend and expand
as they do in the world, elbow, toe, shoulder,
shadow, curve, shallow. I follow words where
they go, and where they go, if I'm lucky,
is a place I didn't know. Maybe
I'm trying to lead when I should be led,
need to trust the hand as if it were tracing
actual flesh, not charcoal on paper
or paint on canvas, but the thing itself.
The body and the ways light falls on it,
the softness of skin in shadow.

Meanwhile, the bodies pile up,
misshapen, on the floor.

today in the garden,
roses flaring, owls flirting
across yards, pecan trees
leafing, everything but the roses
a dozen shades of green.
Today alone is not lonely.
All three dogs lie close by,
eyes closed. Six months
since you died, and last week,
in a downpour, your voice,
as if you were posed at the foot
of the bed, Mississippi-soft
and plainly cheerful:
Good Morning, it said.
It wasn't you, I knew. It came
from my own needy brain,
but I sat straight up, consoled.

GRACE

The man in the waiting room next to me
is speaking of perch and sunfish.
His friend tells him how to smoke cod.
I had been thinking again, just this morning,
of giving up eating my fellow creatures,
deciding whether fish should be on the list.

I'm concentrating on the *Times,* a man's delight
in whales, his photographing them. Snorkeling
near the islands of Tonga, he's greeted
by a humpback calf. It swims so close,
he has to lower his camera. A moment passes.
He feels a tap on his shoulder. Turns.
Peering into his eye is the eye
of the calf's mother, who'd touched him
with her pectoral fin, weighing
more than a ton. The tap is so light, so graceful,
the man knows she means "too close,"
but it's like a finger to the lips.
He begins to swim with them.

More whales on another page. Bulls. Turns out
they're learning each other's songs—the songs
spreading east, Australia to French Polynesia,
melodies from one pod turning up
as phrases in another's compositions. More variety
each year. One researcher says she thinks
it's all about sex—new repertoires
to serenade the cows. This makes me think
of Coco, my canary, who pulls trills
from the outside birds into his April love songs.

If I knew how, I'd combine those whale
and canary notes, then add in
the ones a composer captured from the sun.
Music, we've learned, changes the brain. So what if
someone wove a concerto of stars, elephants,
whales, birds, toads, mezzo sopranos, cicadas . . .
so we'd hear each as part of the other,
and all our brains begin to harmonize.

Still waiting, I doze,
hear armies choiring together,
percussion of carnivores laying down their knives.

Reviewing the Latest Book of a Poet
Whose Work I Once Loved

Once his words carried me through rapids
breathless, wet to the skin, flashing

over falls. Together we were crescent moons
somersaulting dawn.

I ride low now in his new small boat, adrift
on a silent lake—no river, no white water,

and even when a long-tailed bird nests high
and cries, its exotic name seems too much

and not enough.
Like complex dances the muscles

forget, only the gestures are left.
I said. And then

I read those poems again. Their quietness
sneaked into me. A current appeared. I let it take me.
I dreamed the poet arriving in my town,
white-haired, pushing his poems in a cart.

A miracle, a sign, I cried when I opened the door
and he held out a nine-chambered box.

How many times does time reveal the opposite
of what we've believed? How in the in-between do we learn

to love what we'd tossed out?
These chambers might once have held words

explosive as bodies
beyond the reach of ought.

Now, he whispers, they must be filled
with slow discovery, the unwritten, the untaught.

4

*I see fresh cloven prints
under the apple tree, where deer come
nosing for windfalls. They must be
near me now, and having stopped
when I stopped, begin to move again.*
  —Jane Kenyon,
   "Windfalls,"
    Constance

THE UNATTAINABLE

On the paintings of Brian Rutenberg

Somewhere in this house is the only book I care about
right now. I need to study it. I need to see how he creates
saturated landscapes that make me think if I try hard enough I'll find
a fissure in the paint, a rabbit hole of untouched canvas.

It's how I want to paint, I said to my husband.
You can't, he said.
Why not? I said.
Because he's already done it.

Still, when I went to see
the paintings with my painter friend
and mentor, I said it again—

This is what I want to do.
You can't, he said.
Why not, I said.
You can't afford it. Look at the depth
of that paint. Do you know what it COSTS
to use that much paint?
I didn't. But I saw his point.

Still, I long for that splendor,
the pigment so deep you think
you could walk into it, a dream
where everything solid turns liquid
as you enter, you can swim
to the middle, you can lie on your back
and contemplate the sun setting
behind you, its rays warmer
than the water, like living
beyond your life.

Interior with Woman Sewing, 1820s,

Fyodor Petrovich Tolstoy

She looks up from her work to catch
the painter's eye. Green walls, bare floor,
draped white linen curtains at the windows,
even the plants outside on the ledge
suggest Kersting's "Woman Embroidering."
But this is St. Petersburg and her look
welcomes the man at the door—
her half smile says, I'm glad to see you, why
wouldn't I be? (He's the dashing cousin
of the Tolstoy we think of first.) How attentive
he is to her frilly white collar, the way
light falls in her lap, her young plumpness.

Dare we assume the intimacy the scene suggests?
The black, straight-sided horsehair sofa
is less than romantic.
So what is she doing, besides sewing?
She's been waiting all afternoon
as she waits every day, then sits like this,
her neck stiffening while he captures her in paint,
then captures her in an adjoining room, where
he loosens her hair over her shoulders, and the bed
is wide enough to encompass them—but wait—

this is her fantasy, not just ours. Looking closer
you can see that she's hopeful, uncertain,
unused to such close attention. From everything
she's ever heard, this aristocrat will want to ravage her.
But day after day he sets up his easel, paints,
and offers thanks and coins for her time,
once in awhile shares a piece of cake, accepting
nothing to drink but water. This isn't, however,

what she tells her sister. What's the point in spending her afternoons cramped in a chair, a well-favored man alone in a room with her, if there isn't a story?

Nightshirt Sonata

NPR report, April 1, 2011

A white silk nightshirt stuffed in an attic dormer,
the letter B hand-embroidered, baroque,
some musical notes scribbled in quick strokes
on the left sleeve, a paper pinned to the worn

cuff. "Sorry, the ink stain on your boarder's
sleeve wouldn't come out," someone wrote.
It's Vienna. The shirt's more gray than white—old.
Beethoven's? The very thought is enormous.

DNA says yes. Startled from dream,
no doubt, with nothing at hand but a pen—and furious—
he'd written the variations, but not the theme—
then here it came, his brain tumultuous.

Did the date escape me? Did I fall
for it? Oh, Reader, yes. I swallowed it all.

The Little Boat Slips Out to Sea

Again, I feel it rocking, reaching,
tipping toward the garden
I've never seen
at the sea's bottom, where
fish glow against the wheaty weeds,
flower-fish, blossoms
scattering through the deep
like dandelion fluff
from breath.

I'm going, blind
under the dark of the sky,
into night water,
alone in this small
creaking vessel.

I come here
night after night, for what
lives beneath sight, its murmurs
a foreign language, its mountains
a foreign landscape, its lure the lure
of what I can never name.

Too Late

The travel is long and wearying, even
on a train faster than the speed of sound,
which must account for the heaviness
of our bodies. In the new country,
I try to ask directions, tell someone
how far we are from home.
The man behind a counter nods
as if he understands.

      While he's searching
for a common language, you disappear.
I gravitate, as usual, to a café, and there you are
again, listening to yet another sage explain
with only a bit of condescension, where
we went wrong, amazed at how little we know.

Your Death Did Not Sneak Up

It wasn't furtive, it was tough. Seven years,
each cancer trailing the one before,
like sheep on a mountain path,
the ones we often had to stop for
when they crossed the narrow road
in France. Whenever we thought
the last straggler had gone, there came
another, as wooly and dumb as the rest.
When they wandered into open country,
not even the dogs could round them up.

The Seven Villages

Where they were, grass reached
to such feathery heights
on the perimeters,
they were invisible except
by air, if anyone had flown there,
or when wind and rain flattened
the green walls, making them,
for an hour or two, into prairie.
Children might have been seen
from time to time,
tramping narrow paths out
and in, their bodies like flashes
of sun at the edges, bows and arrows
slung over their narrow shoulders.

From somewhere, as everywhere,
soldiers crept up and followed
those beaten trails. They watched
and they waited.

The villagers had guessed at dangers,
but chose the whistling grasses
in seven circles. They lived
in peace, mostly, marrying
into the villages on either side.
They were called by gentle names.
They understood,
without speaking of it, what the end
might be, so every day, after lunch
and the necessary chores,
they spread blankets in the shade,
napped, made love, ate their fill

of berry pies and roasted boar,
and in the evenings invented
dances, and danced.

A Christmas of Cockatiels

I enter the room to the sound of cockatiels
calling. The cage is open.
There should be two, but here are four,
six, eight—wait!—from a cornucopia
in the cage, more cockatiels! Some of them
babies. They shoot into the air like fireworks,
the tangerine moons on their faces appear
in the fig tree. They swoop and descend
like dervishes, swirl through the dining room,
overhead, round the chandelier, whistling—
to each other? To us? It's Christmas,
twenty-four cockatiels, count them,
no pear tree in sight, but anything will do—
bougainvillea, blooming cactus, red begonias
and for the first time, birds
all thriving. I had not forgotten
to feed them, to give them water. For the very
first time, the dream is birds wholly alive, and flying.

You Could Be Drinking Faulkner's Bourbon

eating barbeque
    already living among the stars
        having drifted out of our garden

            beyond the yellow summer roses
    the red camellias of winter

                into the airless beyond

who knows—

    the answer to the interviewer's usual question
      could be drifting toward another galaxy

where millennia from now
    we might embrace in the crossroads of new planets

we tell ourselves we'd like to know   but knowing
    puts a period on speculation
and we are opposed   even in esoteric theory
            to endings

BEGIN WITH WATER CRYSTALS

Mary tells me they shrivel,
lose definition at a growl or the crack

of a pistol. I can almost see them devolving,
amoebic in a moment. *But*, she says,

they reform in the presence of a struck
brass gong—think of the long reverberations—

or the voice of Cecilia Bartoli—
becoming, then, elaborate snowflakes.

I look up the photos. Under a dark
field microscope they could be ornaments,

breath-blown, Masaru Emoto,
who studies them, might say.

Many years ago, plants blackened
in my house before divorce, discord

a high wind howling, setting
leaves adrift.

I read that certain mosquitoes
cannot mate in the absence

of literal harmony. The pitch
made by the male's beating wings, faster

than hers, adjusts as she catches up,
creates a sizzling duet of perfect fifths.

Composer Greg Fox explains how the speed
of sound waves can be divided and divided and divided

by two until the frequencies are audible—
the way he finds the pitch of a planet as it orbits.

I enter my dining room, a sunny garden,
red and yellow Christmas cactus,

bougainvilleas' blushing leaves pressed
to the window, begonias, coral impatiens,

herbs in their small pots, thickening. There,
at breakfast, I listen to "Carmen of the Spheres,"

composed of sounds Fox captured *from within the sun*.
The music slides, reedy, thin, wind chimes

entering my body at angles,
foreign and attuned.

This same morning, listening to the radio, I learn a *ground*
is a repeating bass line. Instruments layered above—

tenor sax, clarinet and flute—
remix the universe,

sound stitching everything to everything.

PRISM

after Arvo Pärt

It requires a rocking, slow, of the right hand.
Light rain, one side of the glass;
flame, the other.

Bow pulled across slowly, like night falling,
a long night in which you do not think.
You do not think of loss.

Pines sway. You are far from everything,
from everyone. Lightness, heaviness,
they become the same.

Lift the air in your two hands. Hold it
awhile. Notice how your fingers
cool at the tips, how the palms

want to keep rising.
There is a lake outside, of course.
Frozen enough to walk on.

And a path through the pines.
You know it's there.
There is no need to go there.

Susan Ludvigson has published ten collections of poems, most with LSU Press. She has received Guggenheim, Rockefeller, NEA, Fulbright, and Witter-Bynner fellowships as well as North and South Carolina fellowships. She represented the US at writers' meetings in Belgium, Canada, France, and the former Yugoslavia. Journal publications include the *Atlantic Monthly, The Nation, Poetry, Georgia Review, Gettysburg Review*, and *Five Points*. Now Professor Emerita at Winthrop University, she also served as poet-in-residence at the University of South Carolina and Appalachian State University. The Library of Congress recorded a reading of her poems in 1995. She is the former director of the Lena Miles-Wever Todd Poetry series.